SURGERY

Tony Hooper

SIMON & SCHUSTER
YOUNG BOOKS

A ZOË BOOK

© 1992 Zoë Books Limited

Devised and produced by
Zoë Books Limited
15 Worthy Lane
Winchester
Hampshire SO23 7AB
England

First published in Great Britain in 1992 by
Simon and Schuster Young Books
Campus 400, Maylands Avenue
Hemel Hempstead
Hertfordshire HP2 7EZ

ISBN 0 7500 1021 5

A catalogue record for this book is available from the British Library

Printed in Great Britain by BPCC Hazell Books, Paulton and Aylesbury

Design: Pardoe Blacker
Picture research: Sarah Staples
Illustrations: Arcana

Photograph acknowledgements

The publishers wish to acknowledge. with thanks, the following photographic sources:

5 Ann Ronan; 6 The Wellcome Institute; 7tl British Medical Association; 8 The Mansell Collections; 9 Ann Ronan; 10 Mary Evans Picture Library; 11b, 12 The Wellcome Institute; 13t Ann Ronan; 13b Mary Evans Picture Library; 14t Ann Ronan; 14b Mary Evans Picture Library; 15 The Wellcome Institute; 16 Mary Evans Picture Library; 17 The Wellcome Institute; 18 Ann Ronan; 19 The Wellcome Institute; 20 Ann Ronan; 21t The Wellcome Institute; 21b Mary Evans Picture Library; 22 Ann Ronan; 23 Trevor Hill; 24t The Wellcome Institute; 24bl Mary Evans Picture Library; 24br Trevor Hill; 25 Ann Ronan; 26t International College of Oriental Medicine; 26b, 27t The Wellcome Institute; 27b The Hulton Picture Company; 28t South American Pictures; 28b Trevor Hill; 29 Ann Ronan; 30 The Wellcome Institute; 31t Trevor Hill; 31b Science Photo Library; 32 Ann Ronan; 33, 34 Trevor Hill; 35t Solo Syndication; 35b Colorific; 36 Frank Spooner Pictures; 37 Science Photo Library; 38 Trevor Hill; 39 Science Photo Library; 40 Trevor Hill; 41, 42 Frank Spencer Pictures.

SURGERY

CONTENTS

WHAT IS SURGERY?

Surgery is the treatment of injuries or diseases by **operations**, which normally involve cutting and sewing. Breakthroughs in surgery have largely depended on developments in medicine. They have also depended on the general advance of science and technology to provide the instruments and tools that enable skilled surgery to be carried out today, generally with little risk to the patient.

DISEASES IN EARLY HUMANS

Since early times humans have suffered from the same sorts of medical problems as we do today. They, too, broke their arms and legs and suffered from the crippling effects of **arthritis** and bone growths or **tumours**. The remains of a primitive ape-man, found in 1891 by Dr Eugène Dubois, show the marks of a large tumour on the inside of the thigh bone.

Other **fossil** records show that the first humans also suffered from dental decay and other diseases, such as **scurvy**. We know this because all of these conditions leave recognizable marks on the bones of the skeleton.

TREATING BROKEN BONES

However, we do not know how these problems were treated. It is possible that, if bones were broken, attempts were made to put them back together again and they were strapped firmly in a **splint** to hold them in place. Some badly-mended fossil bones have been found that show that people did recover from these breaks, or **fractures**. In Australia, Aborigines sometimes partially buried people in sand to hold a broken limb completely still and speed its mending.

HELPING THE PAIN

Treating pain has been a difficult problem throughout time. It was known very early on that the leaves and roots of some plants were useful in reducing pain. The native Indian people of some South American countries have chewed the leaf of the **coca** plant for hundreds of years to control pain and hunger. Alcohol was also used to deaden pain.

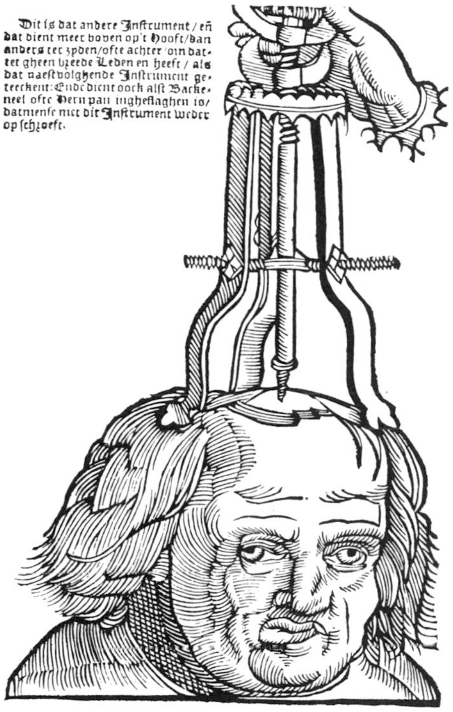
Dit is dat andere Instrument / eñ dat dient meer boven op't Hooft/dan anders ter syden/ofte achter 'om dattet gheen breede Leden en heeft / als dat naestvolghende Instrument geteeckent: Ende dient oock alst Backeneel ofte Hernpan ingheslaghen is/ datmense niet dit Instrument weder op schroeft.

This woodcut, from a sixteenth-century Dutch book about surgery, shows a trephining tool of that time.

Removing demons

No one knows why trephining was performed but some people think that early societies believed that headaches were caused by 'devils' or 'demons' who lived in the head and could only be released in this way. Even today there are some societies which have similar beliefs. They have special people known as witchdoctors, or medicine men, who work to drive away the 'evils spirits' that are thought to be the cause of an illness. In modern surgery, the trephining operation is done to relieve **pressure** on the brain.

The earliest operations

The earliest operation we know of was made on a Neanderthal man about 45 000 years ago. His skeleton was found in the Zagros Mountains of Iraq, and showed that his right arm had been cut off, or **amputated**. Later skeletons, from Neolithic people who existed from about 5000 BC to 2500 BC, showed evidence that an operation was carried out on their head, or **skull**. A circular disc of bone was removed in this operation, which is known as **trephining**. To start the operation a circular groove is cut into the skull. The groove is gradually deepened until the disc of bone can be lifted out. Holes of this kind have been found in many fossil skulls of both adults and children. Some of the skulls show that this operation was made on living people because new bone growth can be seen.

Operations to deliver babies

Another operation that is shown in early records is called a **caesarean section**, from the Latin word meaning cut. This operation was first recorded in India around 2000 BC. Until well into this century, women often died when they were giving birth. It is likely, although not certain, that the caesarean operation was made on pregnant mothers who died during childbirth in a last-minute attempt to save the baby's life. The caesarean section allowed unborn babies to be delivered by cutting open the mother's **abdomen**. During Roman times, the caesarean section was the only kind of surgery that was allowed. According to the law of the time, no woman who had died during her pregnancy or in childbirth could be buried until her infant had been removed by an abdominal cut. The first Roman emperor was delivered this way and was named Caesar. The first caesarean section in which both the mother and the child survived was not performed until AD1500 and was carried out by a pig herder. Today, when childbirth is proving too difficult and the new child's life is at risk, **surgeons** still prefer to perform a caesarean section to deliver the child.

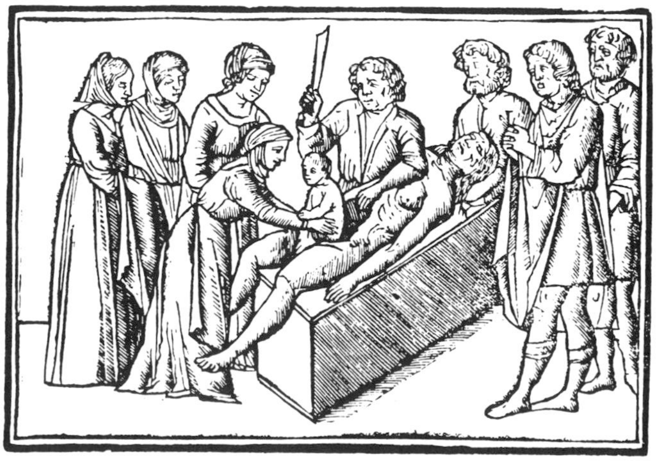

This fifteenth-century print gives the artist's impression of the caesarean birth of Julius Caesar.

THE FIRST DOCTORS

We know that 4000 years ago people who treated diseases and injuries had an important role in society. In about 1760 BC, King Hammurabi of Babylonia, now part of Iraq, made a Code of Laws which controlled how doctors should behave. The code laid down how much a doctor should be paid for treating an **abscess** or saving someone's sight. The payment varied depending on whether the doctor was treating a slave or his master. The code also laid down penalties, which could be as severe as cutting off a hand, if the doctor's treatment failed!

THE ANCIENT EGYPTIANS

The Ancient Egyptians knew more about medicine than the Babylonians. The Elbers papyrus, found near Thebes on the River Nile, dates from about 1500 BC and it contains magic spells and chants designed to cure ailments ranging from eye **infections** to **wounds** from crocodile bites! Despite their magical beliefs, the Egyptians had a fairly practical approach to doctoring and knew how to reset **dislocated** joints, how to immobilize fractures with splints and a sort of **plaster**, and how to **suture** wounds together.

This is part of the Elbers papyrus. The papyrus plant was once common in Egypt and its pith was cut into strips and pressed together to make writing material.

SURGERY

The design of the British Medical Association (BMA) logo includes a serpent. The serpent has been used as a symbol of healing for over 2000 years.

PARTS OF THE BODY

The Elbers papyrus shows us that the Ancient Egyptians also had a good knowledge of all the internal parts of the body, or **organs** such as the **heart, liver** and **stomach**. This was because they preserved, or **embalmed**, dead bodies. However, as they only cut open dead bodies, they did not understand what these organs did. Advances in surgery were held up for hundreds of years by this lack of knowledge about how the human body works.

GREEK TRADITIONS

The Greeks, who became the dominant peoples in Europe after 700 BC, used much of the early doctoring knowledge of Egypt and Mesopotamia, the region around Babylonia. Doctors from these areas were driven by war to Ionia (now in Turkey) and the island of Cos. Here there were temples dedicated to Apollo and Asclepius, two Greek gods of healing. The priests of the temple asked the patients to describe their dreams to them. Then the priests would decide what the dream meant and, using their medical knowledge, tell the patients what the gods wanted them to do. The priests used harmless, sacred snakes in their rituals, and the serpent is still used as a symbol of healing today.

However, the Greeks added new knowledge to medicine when they tried to stop relying on magic for **diagnosing** and healing, and looked for physical reasons to explain illnesses. Between 470 BC and 377 BC there lived two men who had a profound effect on the development of medicine. One was Socrates, who was a leader in this movement, and the other was the most famous of the early doctors, Hippocrates.

THE FIRST DOCTORS

HIPPOCRATES AND HIS MEDICAL SCHOOL

Hippocrates, 'the Father of Medicine', was born on the island of Cos in 460 BC but travelled and practised medicine all over the Greek world. He founded a teaching school on Cos and wrote several books on medicine. Over the next 100 years his school produced about 70 books, all inspired by his example. One of these books was called *The Heart* and attempted to describe the parts of the heart. However, later medical discoveries proved that much of the book was wrong.

THE HIPPOCRATIC OATH

All doctors from Hippocrates' school had to take an oath, now called the Hippocratic Oath, which laid down rules about how doctors should behave towards their patients and what things they could or could not do. In the oath, the doctor has to promise to 'use my power to help the sick to the best of my ability and judgement; I will abstain from harming or wronging anyone by it'. The oath also makes a distinction between the roles of doctor and surgeon by making the doctor promise 'I will not cut, even for the stone, but I will leave such procedures to the practitioners of that craft'. The 'stone' mentioned in the oath relates to stones in the **bladder**. Cutting stones from the bladder was one of the most common operations of that time.

The Hippocratic Oath is still taken by doctors today, although in a more modern form which was written in Geneva, Switzerland in 1948 and revised in Sydney, Australia in 1968. Many of the original principles laid down by Hippocrates remain important today.

This bust of Hippocrates is held at the British Museum in London.

SURGEONS AND PHYSICIANS

It is interesting that the cutting of people for medical reasons, was forbidden to the **physician**, or medical doctor. Physicians often came from the richer, educated people. Surgery was only allowed to be done by a separate, less well-educated group who were seen as **craftsmen**. This is no longer the case in modern times as the surgeon must first train in all the skills of medicine. However, the separation of 'gentleman' doctors from the more lowly craftsmen-surgeons probably slowed the progress of surgery.

SURGERY

THE ALEXANDRIAN SCHOOL

The works of the Hippocratic school were eventually taken to Alexandria in Egypt to form part of the greatest library in the ancient world. These works formed the basis of a new medical school there. After Ancient Egyptian times, when bodies were embalmed, religious beliefs forbade the cutting up, or **dissection**, of human bodies after death, and so nobody knew very much about how our bodies worked. At this time, nearly all knowledge of **anatomy** was based on dissecting animals.

The ban on dissecting humans was lifted briefly around 280 BC in Alexandria and taken advantage of by two physicians, Herophilus and Erasistrates. Herophilus investigated and described the stomach, and timed the heart's beating, or **pulse rate**, by a clock. Erasistrates described the parts of the brain and different types of **nerve**. Sadly, nearly all of the work of the Alexandrian school was lost in the seventh century AD when the library was completely destroyed.

This advertisement shows that barbers of the eighteenth century practised dentistry and bleeding as well as shaving.

Blood-letting, or 'breathing a vein' was still common in the nineteenth century. This print shows a patient being treated for over-eating.

THE FOUR HUMOURS

About 350 BC, the Greek thinker Aristotle had proposed an idea, or theory, about diseases that said people were either **sanguine, phlegmatic, choleric** or **melancholic**. There were four qualities to go with these **humours**. These qualities were cold, hot, moist and dry. Also, all matter was supposed to be made from four things; earth, air, fire and water. The theory of Four Humours, which explained how living creatures worked and what illnesses they were likely to experience, was widely believed for hundreds of years.

THE VITAL SPIRIT

The Alexandrians also followed the ideas of the humours and thought that disease was caused by too much blood in the affected area. This idea persisted and, until recent times, much illness was treated by **blood-letting**, where blood was drained from the diseased areas by opening a vein or by applying blood-sucking animals called leeches! Medical theory thought that air entered the **lungs** and went to the heart where it was changed into a Vital Spirit which flowed to the rest of the body by the **arteries** and the nerves to give the body the power of movement and the capacity to feel.

These ideas were, in the end, seen to be completely wrong. However, they dominated medical thinking for nearly 2000 years without ever being seriously questioned or tested.

HIPPOCRATES AND HIS MEDICAL SCHOOL

THE ROMAN TRADITION

From 146 BC, the Roman Empire dominated most of the western world, including the Greek Empire. In early Roman society, the head of the household learned simple medical skills and acted as a doctor for his immediate family and his slaves. There were no independent doctors as such until the Greek physicians established themselves in Rome. For a while, they abandoned much of Hippocrates' theories of natural healing in favour of the established Roman treatments. These relied largely on herbs and prayers and offerings to the gods.

However, Hippocratic beliefs gradually regained importance and by AD 30 Cornelius Celsus had published *De Re Medicina* (*Of Things Medical*). Celsus's book also described **plastic surgery** to restore noses – which were frequently chopped off in battles, operations to remove stones, **goitres** and **tonsils**, and repair **hernias**. The book was widely read and reprinted and was still in use in Italy over 1400 years later, in 1478!

CLAUDIUS GALEN

The most influential medical figure of Roman times was Claudius Galen who was born in Greece in AD 131. Galen developed the idea of the Four Humours further and gained much anatomical knowledge from dissecting pigs and Barbary apes, as human dissections were still illegal. Galen had been a surgeon in his native Greece before moving to Rome. He was knowledgeable about bones and their joints, but he misled many others for centuries with his insistence on the Vital Spirit idea of how the body worked.

This is an artist's impression of Galen lecturing to his Roman employers.

ROMAN HOSPITALS

The Romans continued the Greek idea that a gentleman should not dirty his hands by actually practising medicine. This task was given to slaves. If slaves fell ill, they were sent to a small island in the River Tiber near Rome, and if any slave recovered he was freed. Freed slaves helped others to get better, and this is probably the first known hospital. The Romans also set up hospitals in the forts and towns that they built to control the countries their army had conquered. Their army (and the navy) took surgeons and physicians with them to work in field hospitals, which they set up wherever they were fighting. These surgeons used instruments that were similar to those still used today. There were knives, or **scalpels**, surgical tubing, **forceps**, and various surgical mirrors.

SURGERY

ALBUCASIS

Surgery made little progress after the destruction of the Roman Empire with the exception of work done by Albucasis, late in the 900s. Albucasis was born and worked in Cordoba in Spain. He was a Moor. Moors were an Arab people who ruled most of Spain until the 1100s. The Moors followed the Islamic religion which had different views on illness from Christianity. Surgery in Cordoba was very basic and restricted to some eye surgery, opening abscesses and setting broken bones. Albucasis was responsible for introducing the idea of applying a piece of red-hot iron to wounds to **cauterize** them and stop bleeding. Cauterization must have been unbearably agonizing in those days when there were no effective painkillers, or **anaesthetics**, but it must also have saved many lives.

Celsus's book made popular Asclepiades' idea of 124BC that diseases were caused by combinations of stresses and relaxations in the body. Asclepiades thought these could be treated by bathing in hot and cold waters. This accounts for the well-known Roman preoccupation with bathing!

EARLY ARABIC SURGERY

The destruction of the Roman Empire also saw the virtual destruction of the medical and surgical ideas of the Greeks and Romans. However, some of the ideas were carried on by Nestorius. He was a leader in Jerusalem, and in AD431 he was expelled from there for preaching **heresy**, or ideas that were against the religious teaching of the time. Nestorius was forced to move away with his followers and they set up schools of medicine in Asia Minor, now Turkey, and Persia, now Iran. They translated the Greek and Roman medical texts into Arabic and kept the Hippocratic tradition alive for the next 500 years, when it was taken up again in Europe. In the Middle Ages, the Arabic texts were translated again – but this time into Latin, which was used by all educated people.

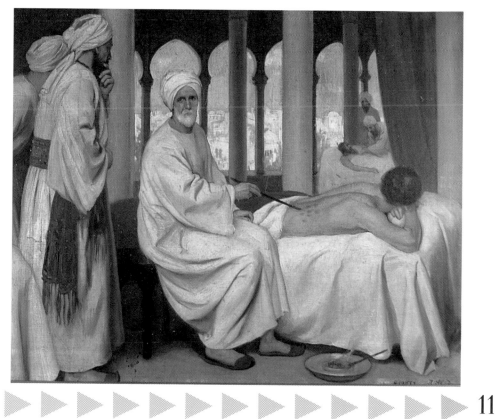

Albucasis is shown here teaching his fellow Arab doctors.

THE ROMAN TRADITION

DELAYING IMPROVEMENTS

During the first thousand years after the birth of Christ, the Christian Church gradually spread its influence all over Europe. The Church, with its belief in life after death, did much to discourage advances in medical healing. It taught instead that illness was caused by God as a punishment for sin, and could only be cured by prayer. Priests and monks were not allowed to study medicine. The Church was against people **researching** into anatomy or surgery, and the entire medical profession fell into disrepute and decline.

THE HEALING SAINTS

The holy people of Christianity are known as saints. Many of these were people who were supposed to have made miraculous healings. The two most famous of these in surgery are the Saints Cosmas and Damian. There is a picture painted by Alonso de Sedano about 1500 showing these saints performing 'The Miracle of the Transplanted Leg'. The picture shows the amputated lower leg of one man being replaced by the lower leg from another man.

This is de Sedano's painting of Saint Cosmas and Saint Damian performing the first known transplant operation.

This 15th-century patient is being prepared for an amputation of his left leg. The fire on the right holds the iron instruments which were used to cauterize the wound to stop bleeding.

THE MIDDLE AGES

After the Moors were driven out of Spain by the Christians, there were no significant advances in surgery in Europe because of the Church's negative attitude. However, the Church also taught that people should care for others less fortunate than themselves, without regard to their colour, class or creed. Many religious groups were set up specifically to care for the poor and the sick. Nursing infirmaries or hospitals gradually grew up around religious groups such as the Orders of St Bartholomew and St Thomas. Today, there are still large hospitals in London with these names.

THE MEDICAL SCHOOLS

A medical school was formed in Salerno, Italy, to help in caring for the sick. It existed there between 1100 and 1300. Although medicine later came to be largely practised by men, the school at Salerno had women on its teaching staff and also as students. Another medical school was founded in Bologna in Italy in 1158. It was followed by a school in nearby Padua in 1222. At Bologna, Theodoric de Lucca reintroduced an effective pain killer. This had been mentioned in earlier medical books and was a small sponge which had been soaked with a mixture of **opium** and **mandrake**, which the patient sucked or swallowed. In 1221, the Emperor Frederick II, who ruled most of Europe, made it law that no one should be allowed to practise medicine until they had completed the course at Salerno. The teachings of the Salerno school were very important for many years.

The mandrake plant. Only the root was used to reduce pain.

BOOKS FROM SALERNO

The doctors of Salerno produced a number of books to explain their ideas. One of the books was on general health care called *Regimen Sanitatis Salernitanum* (*The Health Regime of Salerno*). It recommended moderation in everything and gave programmes of diet, rest and exercise. This book became very popular again in the 1800s.

Another book, which had a great influence on the later schools in Bologna and Padua, was written by Roger of Salerno and called *Surgery*. It was compiled in 1170 by one of Roger's pupils, Guido of Arezzo, and deals with the techniques of trephining, and the treatment of fractures, dislocations and wounds, especially those caused by arrows and swords! Roger's work was based on his own experience as well as translations from the original Greek and Arabic sources. Another basic text called the *Bamberg Surgery*, written in Latin, was based on both Greek and Arabic texts.

The Anatomy theatre at Padua could teach hundreds of students at a time.

MONTPELIER MEDICAL SCHOOL

The medical school at Montpelier in France took over from Salerno in the 1300s and 1400s. Students went there from many countries. During the early 1300s, Guy de Chauliac was one of these. He was a French surgeon and he wrote a book in which he describes operations for hernias and bladder stones and suggested the use of pulleys and weights to keep broken leg bones in **traction**, which kept them stretched and in place. This technique is still used today.

BURNED AT THE STAKE

Even during the Renaissance, it was still dangerous to disagree with the Church. The Spanish **anatomist** Miguel Servede was the first to say that blood passes from the lungs to the heart. He was burned at the stake in 1553 because of this and other ideas that he had written about. His book was also burned with him.

This drawing of a surgeon examining a patient dates from 1497. A knife and ties can be seen on the table.

These heretics were burned at the stake in 1208 by the order of King Philip II of France.

THE FIRST DISSECTIONS

By the end of the Middle Ages, the Christian Church's teaching on medical practice was being increasingly questioned. By 1300, the school in Bologna had special permission from the Pope to begin some human dissection, although priests and monks were still forbidden to practise surgery. For some time public dissections had occasionally been allowed as a form of *post mortem* to discover the cause of death. Like all surgery of the time, these dissections were generally made by a servant under the direction of a master. Mondino de Luicci from Bologna wrote his book *Anatomia* in 1316. He was unusual in that he made many of the dissections himself and did not use a servant to perform the surgery. Mondino's work marks the beginning of a true understanding of the way our bodies work. However, the ban on dissections was still in effect and nothing more was discovered until 250 years later. This breakthrough came in Padua during the period we call the Renaissance.

SURGERY

THE RENAISSANCE OF THE 1400s AND 1500s

The Renaissance was a period of great learning and discovery. It saw the invention of the printing press, which made books more easily available. People became more interested in education and there was a rapid growth of universities and schools that were independent of the Church. The growing numbers of educated people forced the Church to reconsider its teachings on the practice of surgery. This had been limited to unskilled, untrained men who were either servants or whose main occupation was that of barber but who also performed surgery. The changes meant that by 1536, the first instruction book of surgery was written by a Swiss physician known as Paracelsus. Paracelsus had many new ideas on medicine and even burnt the books of Galen whose ideas had been misleading doctors since Roman times. He was a great influence on medicine during the Renaissance period.

LEONARDO DA VINCI

From the late 1400s, Leonardo da Vinci, an Italian artist, dissected over 30 corpses in spite of the restrictions on dissection. As a result of these dissections, he was able to make some 750 detailed drawings of all parts of the body including the **muscles**, veins, arteries and the internal organs. His drawings are remarkably accurate but his work was not published for nearly 200 years, so we do not know if his knowledge influenced people in his own time. He started a new text book which corrected previous mistakes by people such as Galen, but it was never printed.

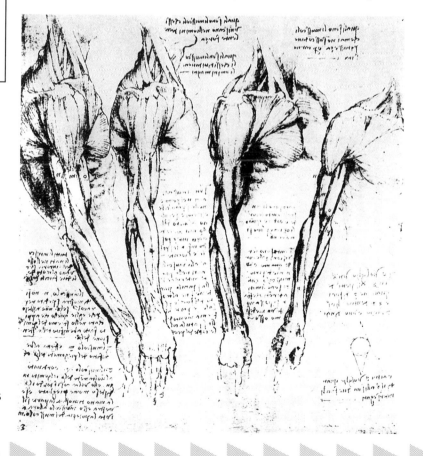

Here are some of Leonardo da Vinci's anatomical drawings of the human arm, shoulder and neck.

ANDREAS VESALIUS

Andreas Vesalius was born in 1514 in Brussels, Belgium. His father was an **apothecary** and his grandfather and great-grandfather were both doctors. He trained as a doctor first at Louvain University and, later, in France at the University in Paris. There he practised dissection on the skeletons of criminals who had been hanged. He stole the bodies from the public gallows at the side of the road. Vesalius later moved to Padua where dissection was allowed. He became Professor of Surgery and Anatomy at Padua in 1537, when he was only 23.

A BRILLIANT SURGEON

In 1543, Vesalius published his great work *De Humani Corporis Fabrica* (*The Workings of the Human Body*). This work had more than 300 wonderful illustrations of the human body and its organs drawn by Jan van Calcar, who was also Belgian. Vesalius showed only what he had seen in his dissections. He was able to correct many misunderstandings passed down from earlier surgeons who had only been able to work on animals. Vesalius often performed his dissections in front of crowds of students. His painstaking results led a group of educated men to take surgery seriously, and gradually surgery was taken from the hands of the ignorant barber-surgeons.

Vesalius was made physician to Emperor Charles V as a reward for his work and made no further contribution to surgery.

VESALIUS'S PUPIL

Vesalius's pupil Gabriele Fallopio carried on his work. Fallopio became Professor of Anatomy after Vesalius. In 1561, he published one of the first books on anatomy in which he described the tiny parts of the inner ear and much of the **reproductive system**. Fallopio also discovered the tubes which carry human eggs from the **ovaries**. These tubes are known today as fallopian tubes.

This picture of Andreas Vesalius was drawn by the illustrator of his book, Jan van Calcar.

SURGERY

AMBROISE PARÉ

In France, while Vesalius was working in Italy, a barber-surgeon called Ambroise Paré was gaining more practical surgical experience on living people. Paré started his career in Paris as a barber-surgeon in 1533, but later became surgeon to Henry II and the three French kings who reigned after Henry II. Paré studied the works of Vesalius to improve his own knowledge.

Paré also worked as an army surgeon and he became expert at treating battle wounds. As France was at war almost continuously for 20 years he got plenty of practice! Unfortunately, he was unable to save Henry II when he was wounded in the head with a lance, despite consulting Vesalius and dissecting four other heads before deciding what to do for the best.

ANNO ÆTATIS. 68

This woodcut of Ambroise Paré dates from 1578 when Paré was 68 years old.

This battlefield scene shows an army surgeon operating on a soldier. The cauldron over the fire holds hot pitch.

THE FATHER OF MODERN SURGERY

Paré was a **humane** man and went to some lengths to avoid surgery unless it was absolutely necessary. Until Paré's time, all amputation had been treated with hot **pitch** and cauterized to stop the bleeding. This caused terrible pain. Paré replaced the pitch with egg yolk and turpentine and introduced the **ligature**, or tying up of the blood vessels, to replace cauterizing. He also made false teeth, limbs and eyes for his patients. These aids were wonderful for their time, but look very primitive to our modern eyes.

PROGRESS AT LAST

The end of the 1500s had, at last, seen some progress in the surgery. The growing understanding of the structure and workings of the human body was speeded by the anatomical studies of Vesalius, and Paré introduced some more humane techniques. However, there was still a long way to go and surgical techniques were still in their infancy.

THE RISE OF SCIENCE

The 1600s saw the beginnings of the **scientific method** where theories were tested by **experiments**. Scientific thinking changed dramatically under the influence of brilliant scientists such as Sir Isaac Newton. Scientific and technological breakthroughs were suddenly happening in leaps and bounds. In medicine, the rules laid down in Greek times were challenged at last. The power of the Church continued to decline, but it was still dangerous for scientists to challenge Christian teaching, particularly when they were concerned with the workings of the Universe. Giordano Bruno, the Italian philosopher, was burned at the stake in 1600 for saying that he thought the Universe was of infinite size.

William Harvey is shown here demonstrating his discovery of the circulation of the blood to the Royal College of Physicians in London.

Antonie van Leeuwenhoek's microscope doesn't look much like our modern instrument. The specimen was moved into place behind the small glass lens by the thumb screw.

TOOLS FOR OBSERVING

Hand-in-hand with the advance of science came the invention of tools to aid observations and experiments. In 1596, in Italy, Galileo Galilei invented the first thermometer. By 1626, Sanctorius of Padua had developed a **clinical thermometer** to record the temperature of the body. Sanctorius also counted the pulse rate of the beating heart and made experiments on the human **metabolism**, or how our bodies turn food and water into energy and waste products.

THE MICROSCOPE

Another essential tool was the microscope. It is difficult to see how the biological sciences could have progressed without this tool. The first microscope was made in 1609 by a Dutch spectacle-maker.

This microscope used a double **lens** to give a greater magnification than a single lens. The microscope was later put to great use by Antonie van Leeuwenhoek who, between about 1650 and 1723, prepared more than 400 lenses and managed to magnify objects by up to 300 times. Van Leeuwenhoek studied living organisms and was the first to see **bacteria**, **red blood cells** and **spermatozoa**.

SURGERY

THE MYSTERY OF BLOOD

For hundreds of years the advance of surgery was handicapped by confused ideas about blood. People realized that blood was essential to life, even though they did not know why. In the 1400s, when Pope Innocent VIII was ill, he had three young people killed and drank their blood as a medicine! Until the 1600s no one knew what blood was or what it did. Many people thought that it was possible to have too much blood and that this caused illness. The blood was believed to move around the body by ebbing and flowing in a great mass, like the tides of the ocean.

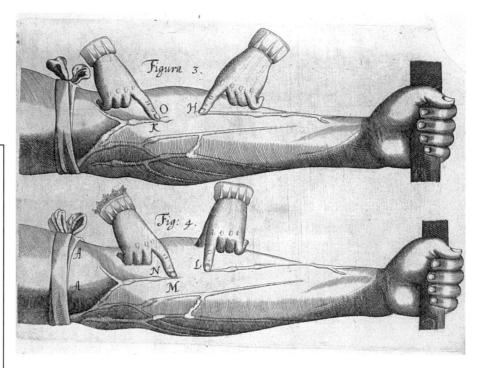

Harvey's book was full of detailed drawings like this one, which traces the flow of blood in an arm.

WILLIAM HARVEY

William Harvey, an English physician and anatomist, studied at the great medical school in Padua for several years around 1600. He was influenced originally by the ideas of Aristotle and Galen but, during the course of dissecting human and animal bodies, he came to believe that the heart acted as a pump pushing blood out of its **chambers** to the arteries and back to the other side of the heart through the veins. He discovered that the veins had a series of **valves**, which only allowed blood to flow *towards* the heart. He also discovered larger valves at the bottom of the arteries which only allowed blood to flow *away* from the heart. This ruled out the tidal ebb-and-flow idea. He published his work in a great book called *Concerning the Motion of the Heart and Blood* in 1628. His work was full of scientific detail and was so convincing that his ideas were quickly accepted.

PROVING HARVEY'S IDEAS

Harvey did his work without a microscope, so he was unable to understand how blood passed through tiny **capillaries** from the arteries and back into the veins. This was explained later by Marcello Malpighi, an Italian anatomist who carried out many microscopic studies of body organs. In 1661, he published *On the Lungs*, which showed the part played by the capillaries.

New Centres of Surgery

During the 1700s and 1800s, the great teaching centre at Padua in Italy was overtaken in importance by new establishments in Leyden in Holland and Edinburgh in Scotland. However, the 1700s also saw a steady rise in the status of surgery in France.

Dominique-Jean Larrey managed to amputate a leg in 15 seconds, thus saving the patient a lot of pain.

THE ROYAL SURGEONS

Surgery became respectable in France through the support, or patronage, of the French royal family. In 1686, King Louis XIV had been successfully treated by the surgeon Charles Felix, and the king rewarded Felix for his efforts far in excess of the fees usually given to the royal physician. Up to this time physicians were considered to be superior to surgeons, so this marked a turning point for surgery. The next king, Louis XV, was persuaded by his personal surgeon, Georges Mareschal, to give money to set up five professorships of surgery in Paris. This was strongly resented by the physicians, who organized a march in protest, but it made no difference.

DOMINIQUE-JEAN LARREY, MILITARY SURGEON

The French Revolution in 1792 and the wars that followed meant that surgical techniques were constantly being practised and extended. One man in particular made a lasting contribution as a military surgeon. He was Dominique-Jean Larrey who was a skilled and humane surgeon influenced by an earlier French surgeon, Paré. Larrey invented the ambulance system to bring soldiers off the battlefield and back to better-equipped base hospitals. Above all he treated all patients according to their surgical need, with no regard for their status or wealth, and showed that he cared for them.

THE FRENCH ACADEMY OF SURGEONS

In 1731, Louis XV went further in improving the status of surgeons when he founded the first Academy of Surgery in the world. This was followed some twelve years later by his rule that barbers would no longer be allowed to practise surgery. Britain passed the same kind of law in 1745, but it only applied to barbers within an 11 kilometre radius of London. The rest of the country still suffered at the hands of anyone who wanted to pick up a knife.

SURGERY

JOHN HUNTER

During the 1700s, surgery was greatly advanced by the influence of one particular surgeon. John Hunter was born in Scotland in 1728. He is viewed as one of the greatest surgeons of all time. He moved to London in 1748 to join his brother William who was already established as a surgeon. William Hunter had founded an anatomy theatre in Windmill Street, which became very famous. John Hunter learned surgery from his brother and others, and then spent some time as an army surgeon when he learned how to treat bullet wounds.

John Hunter

SPREADING SCIENTIFIC SURGERY

Hunter inspired many pupils such as Edward Jenner who promoted the use of vaccination and the aptly named Philip Physick. Physick was an American who studied medicine at Edinburgh and graduated in 1792. He took the knowledge he had gained in Edinburgh and from John Hunter back to America where he introduced scientific surgery and became professor of surgery in Pennsylvania.

EXPERIMENTS AND SPECIMENS

Hunter pioneered a successful method of treating swellings, or **aneurysms**, in the arteries, which are caused by a weakening of the artery wall by disease. He tied the arteries above the swelling. Hunter was also a tireless experimenter who treated surgery as a scientific discipline for the first time. As a result of his experiments he put together a collection of some 13 000 biological and anatomical specimens. This formed the basis of a museum in the Royal College of Surgeons in London until it was bombed during the Second World War. John Hunter published work on several diseases as well as a book on the *Natural History of the Human Teeth* in 1771 and on gunshot wounds in 1794.

Philip Syng Physick was one of the first to use animal ligatures in surgery and to leave them in place to be absorbed. He also invented many useful surgical instruments.

The Tools of the Trade

The explosion of scientific thinking during the 1700s led to many developments that, while not directly related to surgery, helped in its improvement. Greater scientific knowledge increased the understanding of how things worked and the ways in which problems could be overcome. The 1700s and 1800s saw a large number of inventions based on the rise of the scientific method and, as a result, advances in industry and technology. Most of the everyday tools used by doctors today were invented in this period and surgery would not have advanced without the development and use of these tools.

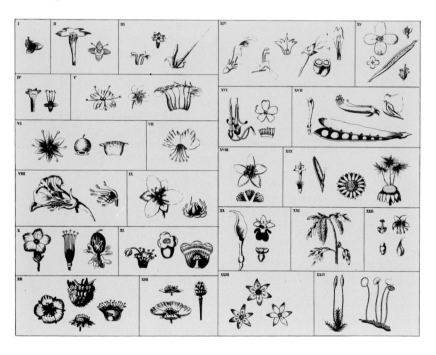

Linnaeus grouped vegetables, flowers and seeds into twenty-four different classes, shown here in a drawing from 1823.

MEASURING THE PULSE

Physicians knew how to use the speed of the pulse as a way of finding out about, or diagnosing, a patient's condition. However, measuring the pulse rate must have been rather hit-and-miss in early times before watches were made with a hand to record seconds. Things were improved in 1707 when Sir John Floyer invented a special pulse watch that ran for exactly one minute, but pulse watches did not become generally used until the 1820s.

GROUPING DISEASES

The system of grouping diseases was developed in the mid 1700s by Carl von Linné, more usually known as Linnaeus. Linnaeus was a Swedish physician who was also interested in botany and started a system of grouping, or classifying, animals and plants. He realized that living things often had common characteristics and could be grouped together. Linnaeus also realized that the same idea could be applied to diseases and he wrote an influential book called *Genera Morborum* (*Types of Diseases*) in 1763. His ideas of classifying became very popular and stimulated a lot of **systematic** scientific research and fact gathering. However, his methods meant that diseases were thought of as separate entities, so doctors believed they should treat the disease, not the person with the disease. Much of medicine is based on this idea. However, today, many people think this approach is wrong and believe that the whole person should be treated. This is known as **holistic** medicine.

SURGERY

MEASURING THE FLOW OF THE BLOOD

Harvey's discoveries in the 1600s about the heart and how it worked as a pump, aroused interest in measuring the amount of flow, or **pressure**, of circulating blood in the body as an extra aid to diagnosing diseases. The first clumsy efforts involved sticking a tube into an artery and seeing how far the blood was pushed up the tube by the pressure. A way of measuring pressure without cutting the patient was devised in 1819 by a French doctor, Jean-Louis Poiseuille and, by 1896, the system we use today was developed. The **sphygmomanometer** used an inflatable rubber cuff. This was fixed around the arm and blown up until the blood flow in the arm was stopped. At that point the pressure of the air in the cuff was the same as the pressure of the blood in the arteries.

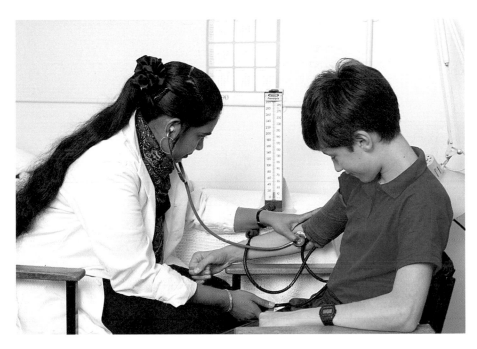

Modern blood pressure measurement still uses an inflatable cuff but the doctor listens to the blood flow stopping and starting again with her stethoscope.

THE THERMOMETER

Body temperature shows whether a patient is healthy, unwell or very ill. Although the Italian doctor Sanctorius had invented a clinical thermometer back in 1626, little progress was made in finding an easy way of measuring a patient's temperature until the 1800s. The 1700s saw the introduction of three thermometers and their different temperature scales. These were invented by the scientists Gabriel Fahrenheit in 1709, René-Antoine Réaumur in 1731 and Anders Celsius in 1742. The three different thermometers were large and difficult to use. By 1850, thermometers had been made smaller and easier to use, but their use in medicine was limited as it could take twenty minutes before the thermometer showed the correct temperature! The thermometer only became widely used by doctors after 1867 when Sir Thomas Allbutt invented a clinical thermometer using the metal mercury. This thermometer was 14 centimetres long and took only five minutes to register.

THE TOOLS OF THE TRADE

THE STETHOSCOPE

Another common diagnostic method involves listening to the sounds made by the body – the beat of the heart or the sound of blood flowing. This used to be done by doctors pressing an ear to the patient's body. This could be very awkward and embarrassing but, in 1815, a French doctor called René Laënnec thought of using a simple sheet of paper rolled into a cylinder. One end of the tube was pressed on the body while the other was pressed to the doctor's ear. Laënnec found this improved the amount he could hear. He quickly improved his basic idea for a **stethoscope** by replacing the paper tube by a wooden cylinder. For a few years the stethoscope remained **monaural**, or for use by only one ear. The monaural form is still used today by doctors listening to the heartbeat of unborn babies.

However, by 1820 the binaural stethoscope, which used both ears, had been fully developed.

LOOKING INTO A LIVING BODY

The last years of the 1800s gave surgery one of its most useful tools – the ability to see inside a body before surgery. In 1895, the German physicist Wilhelm Röntgen was investigating the effect of an electric current passing through a sealed glass tube from which all the air had been taken. Invisible rays came from the **electrodes** in the tube when the

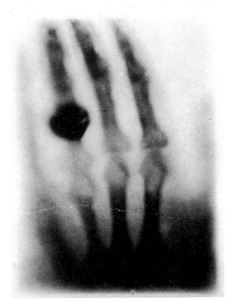

current was flowing through the vacuum. He found that these rays could pass through some lighter materials such as paper, but could not pass through denser objects such as metal. He laid his wife's hand on a photographic plate and exposed it to the rays and took the first **X-ray** photograph. The X-ray photograph clearly showed the bones in her hand and her wedding ring. By 1900, this discovery had been developed into a **radioscope** and was being used as a diagnostic tool by physicians. Unfortunately, long exposure to X-rays is very dangerous. No one knew this for a long time and many doctors became ill until they started wearing aprons made of the metal lead to stop X-rays reaching their bodies.

The first X-ray photograph of Frau Röntgen was taken with an ordinary photograph plate.

This modern X-ray equipment uses much lower doses of X-rays and can be directed exactly where needed.

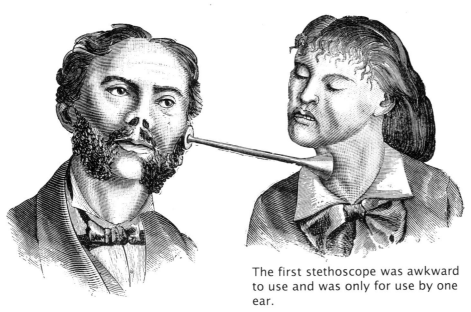

The first stethoscope was awkward to use and was only for use by one ear.

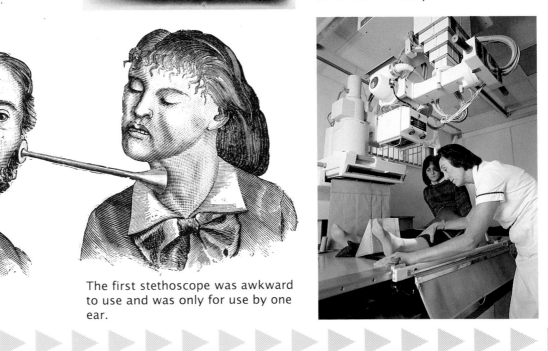

SURGERY

CONTROLLING PAIN

One of the most important factors in limiting progress in surgery was the lack of effective pain control. Without anaesthetics, the operation was too painful and surgeons could operate only for very short periods of time before the patient could endure no more. So surgery was limited to operations which could be done quickly and to those on the surface of the body.

Ether was given to patients from patented inhalers like this.

EARLY ATTEMPTS

Surgeons from early times had used alcohol and drugs made from plants such as the mandrake root to reduce pain. These drugs worked by a general dulling of all the senses but had little effect if the pain was very strong. Also, the amount to be used was never clearly worked out so the drugs were often as dangerous as the surgery itself. So, until the 1800s, even a common operation, such as the amputation of a leg, meant the patient suffered incredible agony, even though surgeons had become adept at performing such operations in less than a minute to minimize the pain.

LAUGHING GAS

The first effective anaesthetic was a gas called nitrous oxide. It was first discovered in 1799 by Sir Humphry Davy. He was an English chemist who discovered many facts about gases. He found that breathing in, or **inhaling**, the gas made people laugh. He also discovered that it made people much less sensitive to pain. He suggested that the gas might be useful in hospitals but his ideas were ignored. It was the laughing effect of the gas that became popular and the gas was used at parties or by entertainers to amuse audiences. In 1838, the scientist Michael Faraday discovered that another gas, ether, also reduced sensitivity to pain, but he too was ignored.

THE FIRST PAINLESS TOOTH EXTRACTION

However, there were some people interested in experimenting with gases for pain control. One was Horace Wells, an American dentist. After he had seen a public demonstration of 'laughing gas' in 1844, he used it on himself while his friend painlessly pulled a tooth out. Wells tried the gas on others but with very mixed results.

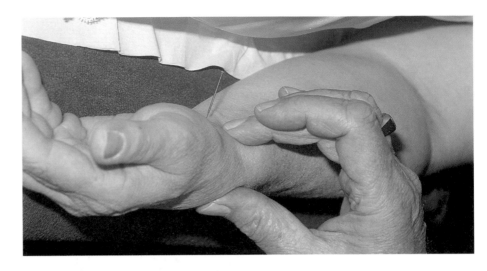

Acupuncture is used to relieve many painful conditions like arthritis. Special needles are passed through key points, apparently without causing any discomfort.

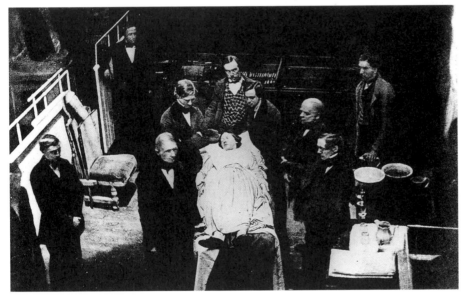

William Morton is shown here with his colleagues from the Massachusetts General Hospital. They are grouped around a patient who has been anaesthetized before her operation.

THE FIRST PAINLESS OPERATIONS

In 1846, Wells' partner, William Morton, experimented on himself with ether and quickly became unconscious. In October of that year at Massachusetts General Hospital, Morton, together with the surgeon John Warren, successfully and painlessly removed a neck tumour from a patient called Gilbert Abbott. Abbott breathed in the ether until he became unconscious and only felt a scratching sensation when the tumour was being cut out. The new process of painless operations was named 'anaesthesia'. Unfortunately, Morton tried to keep the nature of his gas a secret. As a result his ideas did not spread as quickly as they should have. However, in December 1846, Robert Liston in London, amputated a leg painlessly while the patient was anaesthetized by ether. After this, ether was soon being widely used on both sides of the Atlantic.

MIND OVER MATTER

In the 1840s, **hypnotism** was used for pain control with some success, particularly in India. James Esdaile used it in public hospitals on Hindu patients. Unfortunately, he was nowhere near as successful on European patients and his results were dismissed as a fraud by the medical profession. However, it is sometimes used successfully today.

RELIEVING PAIN IN CHILDBIRTH

One of the areas in which doctors were most anxious to control pain was during childbirth. Giving birth could cause a great deal of pain, especially if there were problems which prolonged the labour. The pain often exhausted the mother which made the birth even more difficult. James Simpson was a Scottish **obstetrician** who wanted to find an anaesthetic to reduce the pain of childbirth. In 1847 he held dinner parties where he and his friends experimented with different gases to find the best one! When they tried a gas called chloroform, they 'became bright-eyed, very happy', then very talkative and then unconscious. In fact, they were lucky not to suffer worse effects, because all of these gases are dangerous and can kill if they are misused.

Simpson discovered the anaesthetic effects of chloroform at a dinner party with his friends.

Queen Victoria is shown here with some of her children and grandchildren in 1870.

QUEEN VICTORIA USES ANAESTHETICS

Simpson won the argument for using anaesthetics during childbirth when, in 1853, Queen Victoria accepted chloroform during the birth of her seventh child, Prince Leopold. She was very grateful for the relief and said so publicly. After that anaesthesia became widely accepted.

DISPUTING WITH TRADITION

Six days after his dinner party experiments, Simpson used chloroform successfully to reduce childbirth pains. However, he was soon heavily criticized by leaders of the Church who said it was against the teachings of the Bible to stop pain during childbirth. They quoted the Bible as saying 'in sorrow shalt thou bring forth'. Simpson quoted the Bible back at the churchmen reminding them that, when a rib was taken from Adam to make Eve, 'the Lord God caused a deep sleep to fall upon Adam'.

CONTROLLING PAIN

LOCAL ANAESTHESIA

Chloroform took over as the major anaesthetic for most operations, but, like ether, it was dangerous and sometimes killed the patient. The search continued, particularly in America, to find ways of controlling pain only in the area where the operation was needed. Applying anaesthetics to a small or local area would be much safer than giving a general anaesthetic which made the patient unconscious.

These coca leaves are being sold in an open-air market in Bolivia.

THE COCA PLANT

In the late 1850s, the drug **cocaine** was made from the leaves of the South American coca bush. The Indians of Peru had chewed on the leaves of the coca plant to reduce feelings of hunger or pain for hundreds of years. Cocaine was first used in 1884 by Karl Köller, an Austrian surgeon, as a local anaesthetic during an eye operation. It quickly became popular for use by eye surgeons, but did not become used in general anaesthesia until 1889, when it was used by August Bier in Berlin.

CRYOANAESTHESIA

By the 1600s, a common medical treatment in Finland was to bathe dislocated joints and broken bones with icy water before putting the joints back in place or mending the fractures. This extreme cooling made the operations virtually painless and this idea has been used frequently for local anaesthesia. Modern technology has enabled a similar effect to be achieved by using **cryo-sounds** which can be projected at internal nerves to numb them.

Dentists give a local anaesthetic when they inject your gum to deaden tooth nerves around the teeth they are filling.

KILLING THE PATIENTS!

The rapid spread of anaesthetics in the late 1800s meant that surgeons could now take more time in planning and performing their operations. However, patients still died after anaesthesia was introduced. In Paris 60 per cent of patients died after otherwise successful operations and in Edinburgh 43 per cent of patients died.

This barber-surgeon of the **seventeenth** century is operating on his patient's foot while his son is eating. There is no attempt at cleanliness or hygiene.

RISKY OPERATIONS

Lists of the operations performed by Hunter, his colleagues and the surgeons of the 1800s show that, although there was extensive knowledge of anatomy, operations in the head, neck, chest or abdomen were avoided. This was because operations in these areas almost always led to the death of the patient. Surgeons did not understand why death was so common. However, we now know that these deaths resulted from infection, and shock due to the loss of blood. Until new discoveries were made in these areas, surgery was limited.

PROBLEMS WITH COCAINE

William Halsted did much research work into the effects of cocaine. He **injected** it into himself and his colleagues. Unfortunately, nobody realized at first that cocaine is **addictive** and many of his colleagues were slowly killed by the drug. Halsted himself became addicted but managed to overcome the addiction. To avoid the addictive effects of cocaine, a similar but non-addictive drug called novocain was made. It was in use by 1905.

SPREADING INFECTION

Until the late 1800s, it had always been usual for surgeons to operate in their everyday clothes. No attempt was made at cleanliness and surgeons had even been known to sharpen their scalpels on their leather boots!. Another common practice was for surgeons to perform a *post mortem* on the body of someone who had died, perhaps of a common disease, and then go immediately to another room to perform an operation, often using the same instruments.

A Clean-up Operation

AHungarian doctor, Ignaz Semmelweis, was working in a hospital in Vienna. He became convinced that **puerperal fever**, which killed many women after they had given birth, was an infection spread by the unclean hands of the doctor who attended them. In 1847, he insisted that an **aseptic** or **antiseptic** regime was introduced for his patients. His surgeons had to rinse their hands with a solution of chloride of lime to thoroughly clean them. Semmelweis achieved excellent results with his asepsis and hardly any of the mothers died. However, most surgeons refused to believe that they carried poisons with them and his ideas were largely ignored.

Lister tried **carbolic acid** with immediate results. Deaths after surgery fell immediately from over 40 per cent to less than one per cent. In 1867, Lister published his paper 'On the Antiseptic Principle in the Practice of Surgery ' in the medical journal, *The Lancet*. Unfortunately it was many years before his ideas for healthy, or **hygienic**, surgery were widely accepted by the medical profession.

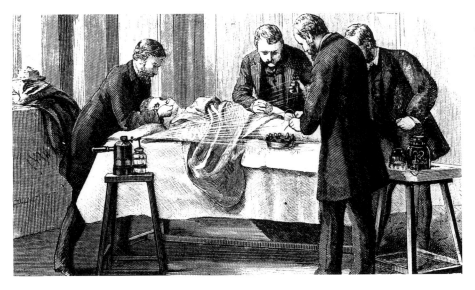

Killing bacteria

Even where aseptic conditions were introduced, patients still died. Most surgeons thought that there was some poison in the air which caused them to die. However, in France, one man made a major breakthrough in discovering the cause of infections. Louis Pasteur was born in France in 1822 and became a professor of chemistry at Strasbourg University when he was 29. Pasteur carried out a lot of work into the decay of food and found out that tiny micro-organisms were responsible for making the food rot or **ferment**. He discovered that it was these **micro-organisms**, or **bacteria**, that turned milk sour. However, if the milk was heated, the bacteria were killed and the milk stayed fresh. Pasteur developed a method for killing the bacteria, now called pasteurization after its inventor.

Joseph Lister

Although Antonie van Leeuwenhoek had first seen bacteria in his microscope in the 1600s, no notice had been taken of his observation. The significance of Pasteur's discovery of bacteria was also not properly appreciated until Joseph Lister learned of Pasteur's work in 1860. Lister was an English surgeon working in Scotland and he became convinced that bacteria carried through the air were responsible for patients' wounds becoming infected. Pasteur had suggested that bacteria could be killed by heating or by using something that was antiseptic as a cleaner. As it was impractical to keep the patients at 60 degrees centigrade, which was the temperature at which the bacteria died, Lister looked for a suitable antiseptic fluid which could be sprayed in the air to kill any airborne bacteria.

THE SPREAD OF HYGIENIC METHODS

Lister's methods and ideas were quickly taken up in Germany where, by the 1880s, Robert Koch had identified the actual harmful bacteria and showed that nearly all of them were transferred by touch rather than by air.

Surgical hygiene meant that the rooms and tools used for operating were kept clean. In 1883, surgical tools were **sterilized** by using dry heat in an **autoclave**, and in 1889, William Halsted pioneered the wearing of disposable rubber gloves.

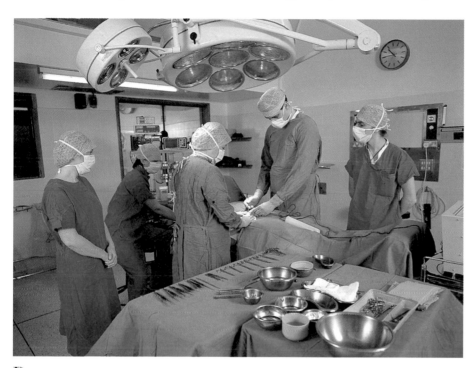

In the modern operating theatre surgeons, nurses and the equipment are all made as sterile as possible to reduce the risk of infection to the patient.

DISCOVERING NEW MEDICINES

For the next 60 years, infections were controlled by keeping bacteria out of the operating area, while treating the patient with a variety of antiseptic chemicals. Some of the most effective were discovered in the 1900s. **Mercurochrome**, which was introduced by Hugh Jones in the 1920s in the US, and the **sulphonamides** came into use in the 1930s. These bacterial agents were only superseded after the Second World War when a new drug called **penicillin** became generally available.

THE INVENTION OF PENICILLIN

Penicillin was discovered by Alexander Fleming, a Scottish scientist. In 1928, he was studying infectious bacteria at St Mary's Hospital in London when he discovered that a green **mould** was producing something that killed the bacteria. He named the bacteria-killing material, penicillin. Unfortunately, he was unable to find a way of making large amounts of it for general use until the 1940s. Since then many other **antibiotics** have been developed to combat bacteria.

Sir Alexander Fleming discovered penicillin, the first antibiotic, in 1928.

A CLEAN-UP OPERATION

CONTROLLING BLEEDING AND SHOCK

As soon as surgeons could control infection and pain, they were free at last to operate in the abdomen and the chest. It then became essential for the amount of bleeding to be controlled. The surgeons needed to do this, not only to prevent the patient from losing too much blood but also so that they could see what they were doing. Surgeons had to be certain that they could make a note of all the arteries and veins that had been cut and be sure that each one was properly sewn up to prevent any internal bleeding after the wound was closed.

SEALING VEINS AND ARTERIES

Ligatures, or tying off blood vessels with knotted thread, was common in the 1800s, but there were often too many bleeding points for this to be done quickly enough. In 1858, Thomas Wells invented a set of forceps that had jaws for holding the bleeding parts together, and a mechanism that locked the forceps closed until a ligature had been tied.

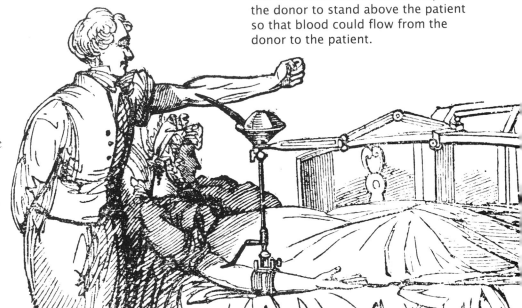

The first blood transfusions required the donor to stand above the patient so that blood could flow from the donor to the patient.

THE INVENTION OF CLAMPS

These problems were eased further by the invention of artery clamps. Two types were invented, one by Jules Pean in Paris in 1862 and the other by Spencer Wells in London in 1872. Their designs are very similar to the modern clamp. In complicated operations today, it is not unusual for hundreds of these clamps to be used to control and mark every bleeding point, and to keep the operation free from blood.

SHOCK

In spite of improvements in surgery, patients were still dying after operations even though pain, infection and bleeding were better controlled. Shock had been recognized as a possible cause of death as far back as 1740 by Henri le Dran. A century later, in 1836, Benjamin Travers published a book on the subject and described its symptoms – paleness, shuddering, a small quick pulse, coldness of the hands and feet, noisy breathing, and unconsciousness followed by death. Travers warned that blood-letting would be dangerous in treating shock. However, twenty years later it was still being practised.

SURGERY

THE CAUSE OF SHOCK

As more operations were performed, particularly during the First World War, surgeons believed that patients were dying in shock either because of a large fall in blood pressure or because of poisons in the blood stream. Both were true in part, but with the rise in aseptic methods shock due to blood loss became the major cause of death after surgery.

ARTIFICIAL BLOOD

There is usually a shortage of blood available for transfusions, so scientists looked for a way to make artificial blood. The first artificial blood was made from petroleum in 1979 in Japan. It was first injected into its inventor Ryochi Naito. In April of the same year, it was given in an emergency operation to a man with a very rare blood group and for whom there was no blood available. By 1986, further research in America had resulted in the invention of artificial red blood cells.

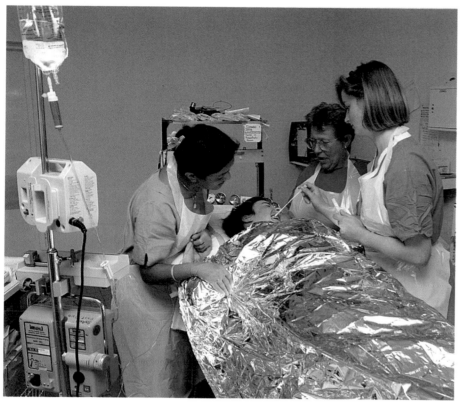

This patient is wrapped in a heat-conserving foil and is being transfused with a saline drip. This is the modern treatment for patients suffering from shock.

BLOOD TRANSFUSIONS

From 1628, when William Harvey had explained how the blood circulated, doctors thought about how to replace lost blood by putting other fluids into the blood stream. In 1667, Samuel Pepys wrote about a **transfusion** of sheep's blood into a man, with no apparent ill effect. In 1818, Dr Blundel of London started to transfer blood from human to human, and in 1829 he saved a woman's life this way. Further experiments in transfusing animal and other human blood caused all sorts of strange and often fatal results. In 1901, the Austrian Karl Landsteiner showed that the problems were brought on because some bloods did not mix but formed clots which then broke down and released poisons into the blood stream.

BLOOD GROUPS

In 1910, Jan Jansky in Prague discovered that there were four basic blood groups and that if only blood from the same group was mixed the clotting effect was avoided. Jansky called the four blood groups A, B, AB and O. However, some people still died when they were transfused with blood of the same group. In 1940, Karl Landsteiner experimented with injecting blood into the Rhesus monkey and identified another factor which differentiated blood groups. This was called the Rhesus Factor, after the monkey.

CONTROLLING BLEEDING AND SHOCK

THE CENTURY OF SPECIALIZATIONS

Since the 1900s surgery has been divided into separate areas that are studied and practised as specialities. Some of these include cardiology (heart surgery), neurosurgery (the brain and nervous system), transplants ('spare-part' surgery), orthopaedics (bone studies), eye and ear surgery, plastic surgery (rebuilding damaged or deformed tissue) and dentistry. Many of these specialities operate with sound and light waves in **sonic** and **laser** equipment instead of the traditional scalpels and clamps. Often these machines allow a completely new form of surgery known as non-invasive surgery, which means that the body is not cut open.

The burned skin on this arm was replaced by new, artificial skin.

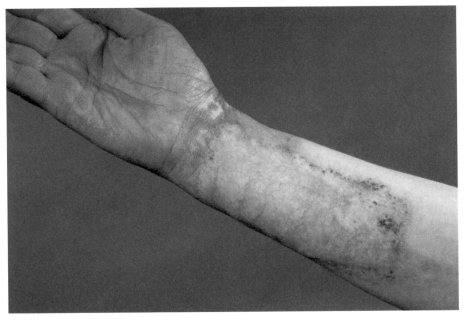

TRANSPLANTS

In the 1600s, members of the Boiani family, who were all doctors, transferred, or transplanted, skin from one patient to another. The skin was **grafted** on to the patient in much the same way as is done today. In 1950, in the US, Howard Green grew some human skin for grafting from a small amount of skin taken from a newborn baby. He was able to grow a piece of skin with an area of 60 square centimetres from a piece measuring one square millimetre in only 20 days. In 1986, John Burke and Ioanis Yannas grafted an artificial skin made from beef collagen and silicone plastic. This skin can be frozen for future use and is easily accepted by the human body.

THE BODY'S DEFENCES

Transplanting other human organs had been attempted for years but without any success. The body has a defence, or **immune** system, which treated the transplant as an invader and rejected the new organ. Many attempts were made to find drugs that could control the rejection, with variable results. However, in 1972, J. Borel, working in Switzerland, discovered that a material from a Norwegian mushroom could be used to **suppress** the immune system and allow the transplants to take. The material is called cytosporin-A and has been used since 1983 in organ and **bone marrow** transplants. There are now frequent kidney transplants and, in 1988, a liver transplant was successfully performed in France.

SURGERY

HEART TRANSPLANTS

Successful animal heart transplants had been made as early as 1964 in the US. However, in 1967, Christiaan Barnard in South Africa made the first successful human heart transplant on Louis Washkansky. Washkansky survived the operation but the drugs used to suppress his immune system allowed him to catch an infection and he died after a few weeks. Barnard continued his efforts and many of his patients survived for long periods. However, the first long-term success was the heart transplant made in Italy in 1968 on Emmanual Vitria who survived the operation by 18 years. The operation is not often performed these days on adults, although heart-and-lung transplants are still made on infants. The emphasis now is on machines to replace the heart.

HEART MACHINES

In 1958, Ake Senning of Sweden invented the first heart machine or **pacemaker**. Unfortunately it suffered from a drawback – the heart could only beat at one fixed rate. This meant that patients were not able to run, or do any strenuous exercise because their heart could not supply a faster flow of blood. In 1986, a German company introduced a pacemaker whose rate of operation depended on the temperature of the blood. As our blood's temperature rises when we use our muscles, the heart beat can rise to compensate. In 1988, the first nuclear-powered pacemaker was fitted. It can remain in operation for as long as 40 years.

Christiaan Barnard pioneered heart transplant surgery in South Africa.

This pacemaker is made of titanium and is normally fixed inside the patient's chest, near the heart.

HEART BY-PASS

As people get older, the arteries carrying blood to the heart can narrow and close. This causes a painful and often dangerous condition called angina. People who suffer from narrowing arteries can have the old arteries removed, or by-passed, and replaced with artificial tubing. In future, this operation may not be needed except in extreme cases because, recently, a drill has been developed which can be introduced into an artery to enlarge it. The drill spins at high speed along the artery and smooths and cleans the walls of the arteries until the original passageway is clear. This operation can be done using only a local anaesthetic.

35

OPERATING ON THE BRAIN

Pioneering experiments which explored the living, human brain had been done in Germany in 1870, when it was found that small electric currents could stimulate it and make the limbs move. This work was repeated and extended on the brains of birds, fish and mammals. In 1880, Victor Horsley, an English surgeon, took the first steps in **neurosurgery**, by operating on the brain.

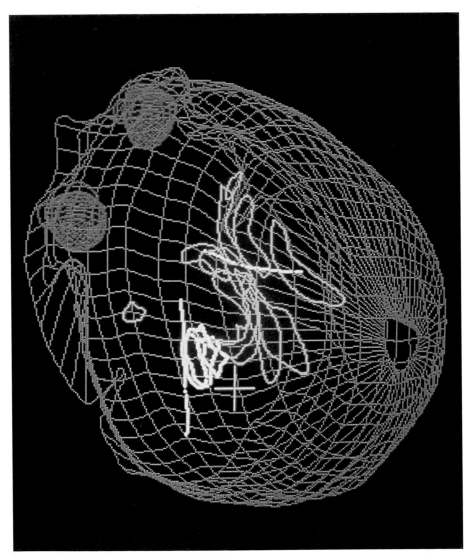

When the brain is operated on with a probe or laser beam, the brain tumour has to be located *exactly* in three dimensions. The cross hairs are centred on the tumour and the co-ordinates fed to automatic equipment to position the beam or probe. In this picture the patient is lying down, the two eyes are clearly visible at the top left.

DEVELOPMENTS IN NEUROSURGERY

Horsley's work was taken up by Harvey Cushing, an American surgeon. From 1900 to 1912, he worked at the Johns Hopkins University developing neurosurgical techniques. He introduced a new style of cut for operations at the back of the skull called the crossbow cut. He also used electricity to seal bleeding points, and started the practice of watching, or **monitoring**, the patient's blood pressure during an operation to warn doctors about the onset of shock.

HORSLEY'S EXPERIMENTS

In 1884, Horsley's experiments on chimpanzees helped to develop methods of operating on the skull and spine of humans. His work also enabled surgeons to predict, from the patient's symptoms, where brain tumours were likely to be found. By 1886, Horsley had made ten brain operations with only one death. Later Horsley made the first successful operation on the **spinal cord**.

SURGERY

Locating the problem

In the 1950s, it became possible to treat some brain diseases by using great accuracy to put a **probe** into the brain to destroy the cells causing the problem. X-rays also helped in locating tumours but the greatest advances in locating and treating precise areas of the brain have come only recently with the invention of **Magnetic Resonance Imaging**, or **MRI**. This machine scans the brain and shows images as slices of the brain on a screen. Any problem area is exactly located and can then be operated on precisely using computer-controlled lasers, **multi-beam radiotherapy**, or sonic waves. These non-invasive methods are used today in preference to the knife.

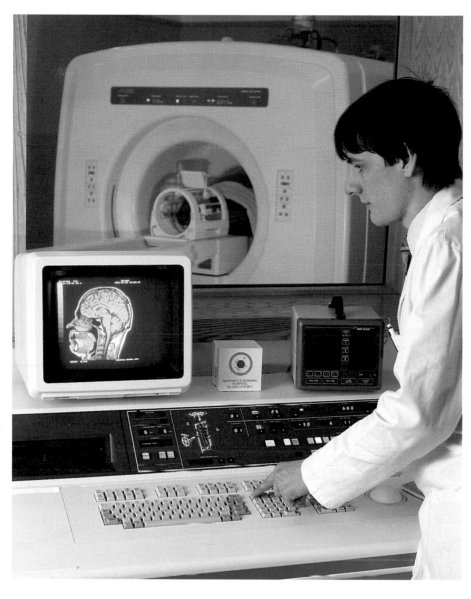

The patient is undergoing a magnetic resonance imaging brain scan. An image of a section of his brain can be seen on the display at the left. You can clearly see the spinal cord and the brain matter.

Balloons are also used to widen arteries which have become blocked. The balloon is guided into place with the help of X-ray images, and briefly inflated to enlarge the artery.

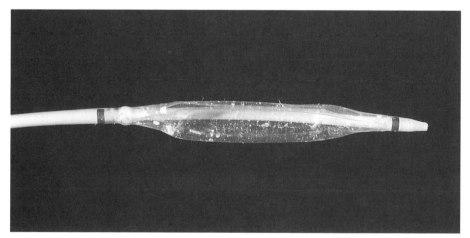

Balloon surgery

Another non-invasive neurosurgical technique, called balloon surgery, was started in 1970 in Russia. After the surgeon has located the part of the brain to be destroyed, a mini-balloon is inserted in the artery supplying blood to that area. When the balloon is in place, it is blown up so that it blocks the artery and stops the flow of blood, which kills the affected part.

OPERATING ON THE BRAIN

MENDING BONES AND JOINTS

The medical study of bones was called 'orthopaedics' in 1741 by Nicolas André, a French physician. Originally, it meant the study of bone deformities in children, but it has come to mean the branch of medicine concerned with all joints and bones. One of the surgeons who specialized in this area was Sir William MacEwen who, in the 1890s, designed a special way of cutting through bone while only making a small cut in the nearby tissue. He was very successful in operating to reverse the effects of rickets. Until well into this century, this was a common disease in children caused by a lack of vitamin D in their diet. It made their bones soft so that they bent easily and became deformed.

FIXING FRACTURES

By 1852, fractures were first fixed by holding the bone immobile in a cast made of bandages and a fine white powder known as plaster of Paris. When the plaster-coated bandages were dampened and wrapped around the limb, they set hard and held the limb rigid. In 1982, an American company developed a bandage coated with a mixture of plaster and **resin**. This made a cast that was waterproof as well as being lighter and tougher.

This X-ray shows a new, artificial hip in place.

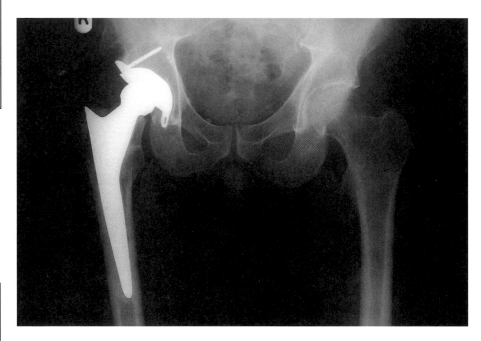

PINNING FRACTURES

Unfortunately, where the bone was badly shattered there were problems in setting the bone in the correct position. However, in 1894, metal screws were introduced to hold the broken parts together. This work was pioneered in England by William Lane, but the metals used were often rejected by the body. When stainless steel was first made it proved to be less of an irritant, and more recently plastics such as nylon and polyethylene have also been used.

REPLACING HIP JOINTS

One area of orthopaedics that has expanded greatly is the replacement of worn joints. Replacing hip joints that have been affected by arthritis is a frequent operation and has been carried out since the early part of the 1900s. In 1938, the metal vitallium was used to give a longer life to the replacement part. Recent developments in materials and the use of computers to design the hip joint to exactly match the old socket, have improved the operation even further. A hip replacement joint is now expected to last twenty years or more. Artificial joints have also been developed to replace the elbow and shoulder joints.

SURGERY

EYES, EARS AND TEETH

The operation to remove **cataracts** was radically changed in 1976 when the American Charles Kelman used **ultrasound** to shatter the clouded lens. The pieces were then removed through a tiny cut in the eye. The lens in the eye was replaced by an artificial lens first invented in 1952 in England by Harold Ridley. Only long distance vision was clear using this artificial lens, so people had to wear spectacles for close work, such as reading. However, in 1989, a lens was introduced in the US which had a variable **focal length**, so both long and short distances are in focus. This should mean that spectacles are no longer needed after cataract operations.

The surgeon is operating deep within the human ear to vaporize a tumour. He is looking through the microscope and directing the laser beam through a funnel to allow the beam to reach the inner ear.

IMPROVING HEARING

If people have hearing problems, they can sometimes be helped by surgery. Our understanding of the ear has grown, notably through the work of Georg von Békésy in the US, on how the inner ear works, so it has become possible to make artificial ear parts, such as the **cochlea**. When first used in 1973 it helped some profoundly deaf people hear muffled sound for the first time. By 1981, technology had progressed so far that the Australian Graeme Clark was able to make the first so-called 'bionic ear'. In 1988, this was successfully implanted in a five year-old girl who had been totally deaf from birth.

ADJUSTING THE CORNEA

The cornea is the membrane covering the front of the eye. With age or disease the cornea can become stiff, and this affects the focusing of the eye. After 1949, a new cornea from the eyes of a donor was sometimes grafted on. In 1979, a Russian, Sviatoslov Fiodorov and a group of other doctors used a new treatment on 22 000 patients in one year. He used small cuts around the edge of the cornea but there is some concern today over the long term benefits of his operation. In 1991, a new technique was introduced in England where the cornea is weakened by lasers.

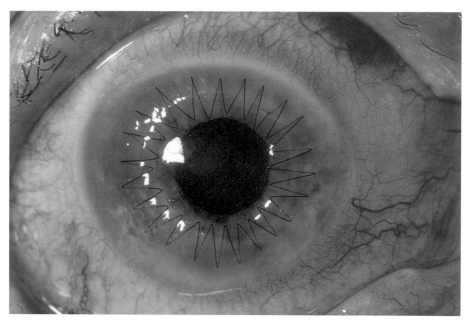

This shows an eye after corneal grafting, with a ring of stitches holding the cornea in position.

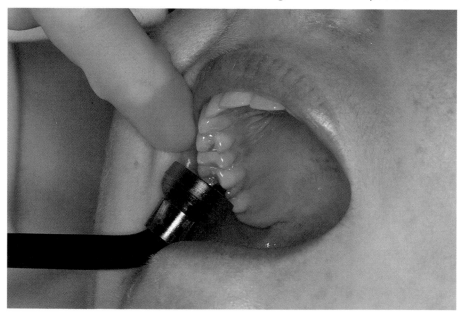

THE DRILL

The major tool of the modern dentist, the drill, was invented in a primitive form by the Roman surgeon Archigenes. Various mechanical improvements were made over the years, particularly in the 1800s. The first high speed drill was invented in 1871 in the US. Today, drills are driven by air and reach speeds of 40 000 rpm (revolutions per minute) and there are drills that work with a laser.

The dentist is hardening the new tooth resin with the blue light.

DENTAL SURGERY

Dental surgery is experienced by almost everyone. Filling cavities in the teeth prevents further decay. As early as the 800s, the Arab doctor Abu Ibn Masawaih filled teeth using solid gold. Gold was used until the 1900s when other **amalgams** were introduced. These blended in better with normal tooth **enamel**. In 1963, a synthetic resin was invented that could be used to rebuild teeth. This can now be moulded in the mouth to the shape of the original tooth and then hardened with an intense blue light beam.

TOOTH IMPLANTS

In 1965, a Swede called Per Ingvar Branemark, invented a method of replacing individual teeth. He inserted a metal peg into the jaw and screwed an artificial tooth on to the peg. This treatment is now offered (at some cost) by most dentists.

SURGERY

PLASTIC SURGERY

Plastic surgery means reshaping or repairing the body using skin, bone and **cartilage** taken from other parts of the body. In about AD 350, Amynthas, of the Alexandrian School, used plastic surgery techniques to repair noses that had been badly injured in battle. However, no real advances in this field of surgery were made until the late 1890s. During this time, plastic surgery to improve the shape of noses, for **cosmetic** effect only and not just for medical reasons, was developed both in the US and Germany. Since then the cosmetic side of this type of surgery has grown and is used on every part of the body from the face to the breasts.

Modern plastic surgery is also used for cosmetic reasons. This woman's nose and chin have been remodelled.

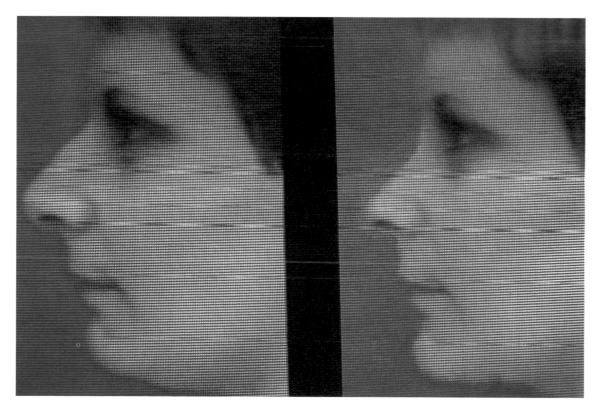

ARCHIBALD MCINDOE

Cosmetic surgeons have drawn heavily on the pioneering work done during and after Second World War by Archibald McIndoe. Born in New Zealand, he studied surgery in the US until 1931 when he moved to England to practise plastic surgery. He concentrated on treating people with skin defects such as birthmarks or severe burns. In 1939, at the beginning of the Second World War, he was in charge of plastic surgery for the Royal Air Force. He performed wonders in restoring faces and limbs that had been destroyed by fires in burning aircraft. Some patients needed as many as forty skin-grafting operations.

MICROSURGERY

The tip of this surgical needle has a cutting edge to reduce damage to the skin. The thread is clamped to the other end of the needle. The photograph is magnified seven times.

Modern technology allows surgery to be carried out successfully even in the most awkward areas of the body. The equipment invented in earlier times formed a foundation for the superb **electronic** surgical instruments used today. Electron-microscopes that can magnify thousands of times, computers and ultrafine needles even enable surgeons to re-attach severed limbs. Technology has refined the curved needles used by surgeons to be as thin as a human hair, with thread that is far finer. To use such tiny instruments, computer-controlled robotic hands can be used and the surgeon views the work through a powerful microsope.

In the past, operations to sew back severed limbs were always failures as every nerve, vein and capillary needs to be reconnected if the hand or foot is to function properly. Extremely fine instruments have now been developed for this delicate work. The operations are so complicated that it can take 19 hours to sew a hand back and the surgeons work in relays. To cut down the operating time, microscopes have been designed so that two or three surgeons can work at the same time to reconnect one severed limb.

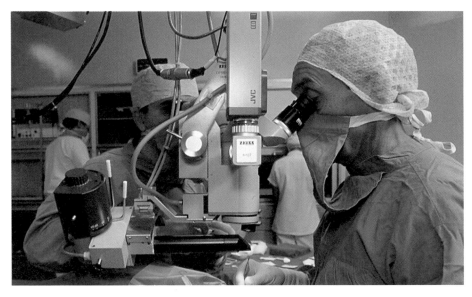

THE FUTURE

Through the centuries many of the problems of surgery have been overcome. However, as technology makes ever-better instruments, the nature of surgery is gradually changing. The trend is towards performing operations without cutting the body. Laser surgery enables light to make bloodless operations in the depths of the brain and even in the ear. The laser beam is used instead of the traditional scalpel and actually **vaporizes** the unwanted tissue. Because the laser light can be directed down thin optical fibres, the surgeon can operate anywhere the fibre can go. So, surgeons can operate inside arteries, in the heart, deep in the brain and on the eye. This non-invasive surgery means that patients are much less likely to suffer from loss of blood and shock and can recover much more rapidly.

KEY DATES

2000 BC Code of Hammurabi of Babylon makes rules for doctors

1500 BC Elbers papyrus shows medical knowledge

460-370 BC Hippocrates alive. Famous for the Hippocratic Oath

310 BC Medical school established in Alexandria

AD 30 Celsus writes *De Re Medicina*

131-201 Galen, influential Roman physician, alive

303 Saints Cosmas and Damian, physicians, martyred

738 Medical school at Montpelier, France, set up

936-1013 Arab doctor, Albucasis, practises medicine in Spain

1100 Salerno medical school becomes established

1137 St Bartholomew's Hospital established in London

1231 Salerno medical school given extra status

1500 Jacob Nufer performs first caesarean operation when mother and baby survive

1505 Charter given to Royal College of Surgeons, Edinburgh

1536 Paracelsus (1493-1541) writes *Chirurgia Magna*

1540s Ambroise Paré (1510-1590) military surgeon, working in France

1543 Andreas Vesalius (1514-1564) publishes *De Humani Corporis Fabrica* a study of human anatomy

1550 Anatomy theatres established in many places

1561 Gabriele Fallopio (1523-1562) publishes anatomy studies

1614 Santorio Sanctorius (1561-1636) publishes his findings on metabolism

1626 Sanctorius records use of his newly invented clinical thermometer

1628 William Harvey (1578-1657) publishes his work on the circulation of the blood

1661 Marcello Malpighi (1628-1694) demonstrates the role played by capillaries

1683 Antonie van Leeuwenhoek (1632-1723) sees bacteria with his microscope

1731 Louis XV sets up the first Academy of Surgeons in France

1763 Linnaeus's (1707-1778) classification of diseases

1800 Royal College of Surgeons (England) established

1819 René Laënnec (1781-1826) publishes work on listening to the chest

1846 Robert Liston (1794-1847) uses ether anaesthesia for an amputation

1847 Ignaz Semmelweis (1818-1865) introduces asepsis

1853 Queen Victoria accepts chloroform during childbirth

1864 Joseph Lister (1827-1912) uses carbolic spray to kill germs

1890 William Halsted (1852-1922) introduces rubber gloves for surgery

1895 Wilhelm Röntgen (1845-1923) discovers X-rays

1900 Neurosurgery developed

1901 Karl Landsteiner (1868-1943) discovers blood groups

1913 American College of Surgeons established

1913 First electron-microscope developed

1928 Alexander Fleming (1881-1955) discovers penicillin

1940 Landsteiner and others find Rhesus factor in blood

1946 Nuclear magnetic resonance invented

1950 Human skin grown for grafting

1958 Pacemaker invented in Sweden

1963 First human liver transplant

1967 First heart transplant performed by Christiaan Barnard (1922-)

1970 Balloon surgery developed in USSR

1979 Artificial blood made by Riochi Naito in Japan

1986 Artificial skin made and successfully grafted

BIBLIOGRAPHY

A Hundred Years of Medicine Wyndham E B Lloyd (Gerald Duckworth and Co Ltd 1968)

An Outline History of Medicine Philip Rhodes (Butterworth 1985)

Disease and Medicine R W Johnson (B T Batsford 1967)

How is it Done? (Readers Digest 1990)

Medicine in History David Storr (Wayland (Publishers) Ltd 1985)

The Body in Question Jonathan Miller (Jonathan Cape 1978)

The Book of Inventions and Discoveries ed. Valérie-Anne Giscard d'Estaing (Macdonald Queen Anne Press 1991)

The Human Body The Editors of Time-Life Books (Time-Life Books 1990)

The Story of Medicine Vernon Coleman (Robert Hale 1985)

Twenty Names in Medicine Eleanor van Zandt (Wayland (Publishers) Ltd 1987)

SURGERY

GLOSSARY

abdomen: the lower half of the main part of the body

abscess: an infected swelling in the body

addictive: a substance that, if taken, makes the body unable to do without it. Many drugs are addictive

amalgam: a blend of soft metals

amputate: to cut off, especially applied to legs and arms or parts of them

anaesthetic: a substance that has the effect of making a person or animal unaware of pain, either by making them unconscious or deadening part of them

anatomist: someone who studies the structure of the body by dissection

anatomy: the study of the structure of the body

aneurysm: the expanding or swelling of an artery

antibiotic: able to kill micro-organisms which cause disease

antiseptic: a substance that destroys germs

apothecary: someone who prepares and sells medicines

artery: a tube that carries blood away from the heart

arthritis: an inflammation and swelling of the joints between the bones

aseptic: when there are no germs present. An operating theatre is kept aseptic so germs cannot harm the patient

autoclave: a strong closed oven or vessel which works at temperatures high enough to guarantee all germs are destroyed. Instruments and clothing used in an operation can be put inside

bacteria: single-celled organisms found everywhere. Some cause diseases

bladder: a small bag in the body that holds waste liquid

blood-letting: making a cut in a vein to let out some blood. It was based on the idea that the body could have too much blood

bone marrow: substance found in the centre of bones. Red blood cells are made in the bone marrow

caesarean section: an operation where a mother's abdomen and uterus are cut open to remove a baby before it is born. This operation is done to save the baby's life

carbolic acid: a germ-killing acid made from coal-tar

capillaries: very tiny tubes that allow blood from the arteries to pass through the body and return to the veins

cartilage: a firm flexible substance similar to soft bone, found between bone joints

cataracts: a condition where the lens in the eye becomes cloudy and doesn't allow light through

cauterize: to burn with a hot iron to destroy tissue and seal blood vessels

chamber: an enclosed space or small room. The heart has four chambers

choleric: having a short temper, being of angry temperament

clinical thermometer: an instrument used to measure the temperature of the body

coca: a small bush that grows in the mountains of South America. The leaves contain a drug

cocaine: a very addictive drug that is made from a substance extracted from the leaves of the coca plant

cochlea: a tiny part of the inner ear. The cochlea has a distinctive spiral shape

cosmetic: purely for appearance

craftsmen: people who do very skilled work with their hands

cryo-sound: sound waves used in low temperature surgery

diagnose: to study someone who is ill to decide what is wrong

dislocate: to put out of place. When a bone slips or is knocked out of place, it is dislocated

dissection: to cut up carefully to examine the structure of something

donor: someone who gives something

electrodes: a piece of metal through which an electric current enters and leaves any machine or electrical device

electronic: something that works by using electrically-charged particles called electrons

enamel: a very hard shiny substance that forms the outer part of teeth

embalm: preserving a dead body by filling it with special chemicals

experiment: a controlled test to find out what happens. Records of what happens are usually taken

ferment: to change as a result of chemical action from yeasts or bacteria

focal length: the focus point of a lens, where light is concentrated so the eye can see the image clearly

fossil: the preserved remains of ancient living things. Usually found in rocks

forceps: an instrument designed to hold an object firmly but without causing any damage

fracture: a break in a bone or any rigid object

goitre: a large lump in the neck caused by an enlarged thyroid gland

graft: to attach something, such as skin, from one place to another

heart: an organ made of muscle which contracts and expands continuously to push blood around the body

heresy: an idea that goes against the accepted teaching of a religion

holistic: a theory that in diagnosis the whole body must be looked at, not just part

humane: having kindness and sympathy for those who are suffering

hygienic: something that is healthy

hypnotism: the study of hypnosis when people's minds can be put into a sleep-like condition and they are less aware of pain

immune: able to resist disease

infection: a disease caused mainly by germs

inhale: to breathe in

inject: to force fluid into a body through the skin

kidney: one of two parts of the body that clean the blood and make urine

laser: a machine that produces a concentrated beam of light so strong it can be used to cut

lens: a transparent piece of material, usually glass, that focuses light in a particular way, often used to magnify

ligature: anything that is used to tie or bind up

liver: a large organ in the body that helps change chemicals in the body to clean the blood

lungs: large organs inside the rib cage which take oxygen into the body by drawing in air

Magnetic Resonance Imaging (MRI): an electronic method of examining the inside of the body without cutting it

mandrake: a plant related to the potato family

melancholic: having a sombre and depressed temperament

mercurochrome: a strong medical compound created from mercury

metabolism: the processes in the body by which substances, such as food, are changed

micro-organism: a living thing that is so tiny it can only be seen under a microscope

miraculous: something unusual that happens without anyone being able to explain it. Supernatural

monitor: to observe carefully and continuously check anything that might go wrong

monaural: using one ear only

mould: tiny fungi growing on vegetable or animal material. Moulds help the material to rot away. They usually appear as a furry mass

multi-beam radiotherapy: treatment using different sorts of invisible rays

muscles: fibres in the body that expand and contract to allow movement

nerves: fine fibres in the body that carry signals to and from the brain

neurosurgery: surgery on the brain, spinal cord and nerves

operations: any medical procedure that involves cutting, removing, repairing or destroying part of the body

opium: a drug that is obtained from the seed pod of a species of poppy

organ: a complete part of any animal body

organism: anything that is living and that can have a separate existence

ovary: the part in the female body where eggs are stored

pacemaker: a small device that can keep a heart beating regularly

penicillin: a powerful drug that destroys bacterial infections.

phlegmatic: having a calm temperament

physician: someone qualified in treating illness with medicines

pitch: a thick, black sticky substance extracted from coal or wood

plaster: a white mineral called gypsum that has been finely crushed. It swells and hardens when water is added

SURGERY

plastic surgery: surgery performed to repair or reshape parts of the body

post mortem: means after death. An examination of a dead body

pressure: a force that pushes on something. The pumping of the heart pushes blood around the body

probe: an instrument that can enter a small space to explore

puerperal fever: an infection in the uterus occurring after childbirth

pulse rate: the rate at which the heart beats. The average pulse rate of a resting adult is 60-80 beats per minute

radioscope: a machine designed to take X-ray photographs

red blood cell: or red corpuscle, that carries oxygen around the body

reproductive system: the method by which each living thing creates young

research: to investigate something to find new information

resin: a sticky substance obtained from trees and plants

sanguine: always expecting the best, having a hopeful temperament

scalpel: a very sharp, small bladed knife used for operations

scientific method: making carefully recorded observations and experiments

shock: a sudden collapse of the bodies' systems due to a severe physical or mental happening, such as a motor accident

skull: the bones of the head. The skull protects the brain

sonic: to do with sound

spermatozoa: or sperm, tiny organisms in fluid produced by male animals and humans, which make the female produce young

sphygmomanometer: an instrument for measuring the pressure of blood in an artery. *Sphygmos* is Greek for pulse

spinal cord: the bundle of nerves leading from the brain, down the back inside the spine bone, to reach the rest of the body

splint: a stick or something similar that is strapped to something, such as an arm, to give it support when it is broken

sterilize: to make free from germs

stethoscope: an instrument for listening to the chest. *Stethos* is Greek for chest

stomach: a large, bag-like organ at the bottom of the ribs where food begins to be digested

sulphonamides: a group of chemicals that destroy bacteria

suppress: to hold down or hold back, to make less effective

surgeon: someone who treats injuries and diseases by cutting and stitching

suture: stitching done on a severe wound to hold the sides together while it heals

systematic: doing something in a very ordered way

theory: an idea based on reasoned thinking to explain certain facts

tonsil: either of two lumps at the back of the mouth. They help fight infection

traction: pulling gently on a bone to help it heal in the correct position

transfusion: to transfer blood from one person to another

trephining: cutting a hole in the skull. Sometimes called trepanning

tumour: an unwanted growth anywhere on the body

ultrasound: sound waves that cannot be heard by the human ear. They can be used to kill cells or to see inside objects

valve: a device that allows liquids to flow only one way

vaporize: to destroy by reducing to minute particles

vein: a tube that carries used blood back to the heart

wound: any injury to the body where the skin and flesh are broken

X-ray: invisible light rays that are able to pass through many objects, except bone or metal

GLOSSARY

INDEX

SURGERY